T0088916

The Bread and the Wine

Evidence of God's Faithfulness in the Waiting

Erin Gregory

WESTBOW
PRESS®
A DIVISION OF THOMAS NELSON
& ZONDERVAN

Copyright © 2020 Erin Gregory.

All rights reserved. No part of this book may be used or reproduced by any means, graphic, electronic, or mechanical, including photocopying, recording, taping or by any information storage retrieval system without the written permission of the author except in the case of brief quotations embodied in critical articles and reviews.

WestBow Press books may be ordered through booksellers or by contacting:

WestBow Press
A Division of Thomas Nelson & Zondervan
1663 Liberty Drive
Bloomington, IN 47403
www.westbowpress.com
844-714-3454

Because of the dynamic nature of the Internet, any web addresses or links contained in this book may have changed since publication and may no longer be valid. The views expressed in this work are solely those of the author and do not necessarily reflect the views of the publisher, and the publisher hereby disclaims any responsibility for them.

Any people depicted in stock imagery provided by Getty Images are models, and such images are being used for illustrative purposes only. Certain stock imagery © Getty Images.

Illustrations by Talia Ball

Scriptures taken from the Holy Bible, New International Version®, NIV®. Copyright © 1973, 1978, 1984, 2011 by Biblica, Inc.™ Used by permission of Zondervan. All rights reserved worldwide. www.zondervan.com The "NIV" and "New International Version" are trademarks registered in the United States Patent and Trademark Office by Biblica, Inc.®

ISBN: 978-1-9736-8998-0 (sc)
ISBN: 978-1-9736-8999-7 (hc)
ISBN: 978-1-9736-9000-9 (e)

Library of Congress Control Number: 2020914786

Print information available on the last page.

WestBow Press rev. date: 11/04/2020

Contents

Preface

This collection of poems was written over a span of more than 15 years and explores a wide range of topics. I began writing initially as an outlet for grief; a way to distance myself from my own sense of loss and to examine it more objectively. With time, I found that writing also allowed beauty to be brought into magnified focus and provided a treasury for cherished memories. It reminded me that in times of need and in times of abundance, God both sustained and blessed me with the bread and wine of fellowship with Him.

The Calling. Our Heavenly Father calls all of His children to draw near and hear His beautiful plan for them. The challenge is to listen, to believe and then to act. My prayer is that we develop ears to hear, hearts to believe, and the courage to act. Imagine!

The North. Written during the years that my family and I lived in Peace River, Alberta, these poems reflect my struggle to find peace and rest in the midst of caring for 3 young children and working as a family physician in a remote, rural community.

The South. Moving to Vancouver Island, British Columbia heralded a time of refilling and refreshing for me. Many of these poems were written in remembrance of God's faithfulness and provision; and others acknowledge our ongoing existence in the not-yet; awaiting the fulfilment of God's promise of a new kingdom.

The In-Between Spaces. Being far from home provides an opportunity to reflect on the past, the present and the future, and is, if we choose, heart and mind expanding. These poems were written while away; to record what I had learned; in the hope that I would return and remember.

The Returning. After years of wrestling with God and struggling to understand His purposes, these most recent poems are birthed from a place of new hope and faith, as I continue to learn to lean on the One who loves me.

The Calling

For we are God's handiwork, created in Christ Jesus to do good works, which God prepared in advance for us to do. Ephesians 2:10

Revelation

Can this be true?
This revelation,
this gift of knowledge?
Who is there to refute it?
Who will deny
that a Father
can speak
to His daughter?

Listen

I love you.
I have only your best interests in mind.
I can bring you to a place of peace.
I can be your true joy.
I want you to be with Me.
I want to splash
My glory all over you.
I want to see you shine.

You don't need to be afraid.
You don't need to shrink back.
You don't need to feel unworthy.

I am the One
who gives you worth,
and I am glorious!

I know your short comings.
I have seen where you fail,
but My love never fails—
My love is so big!

You can jump
and I will catch you.
Leap for joy,
for I am your provider.
I will not let you fall.

Listening

Teach me, Father.
I am willing to learn.
Speak tenderly to me;
I am listening.

I want to hear
Your voice speaking—
telling me,
turn to the right,
or to the left.

Keep me safe from evil
of my own doing.
Protect me from deception—
from the cunning of others.

Help me to speak boldly,
when I need to be brave.
Help me to whisper gently,
when I need to be kind.

Freedom Calling

Innocence in this,
without ignorance.

Freedom!
Freedom!
Freedom!

I cannot be tied down;
I will not be muzzled.

There will be the voice
of a lion roaring.
There will be the sound
of waves crashing.
The wind will howl.
The ground will shake.

I will not be silent
in the face of injustice.
I will *say to the captives "Come out,"
and to those in darkness, "Be free!"*

My mouth belongs to the Lord.

Isaiah 49:9

Sowing Seed

I have been seeking;
wanting to know
what my Father wants.

Creation proclaims
His love of
redemption,
His passion for
making things new.

To what wonders,
to what delights,
of rebirth
have I been blind?

Lulled into complacency,
hushed by the serpent,
rocked by the worries
of the world.

But my Father calls to me.
He tells me He wants
me to write
what I hear.
He tells me it will be
all about beauty.
He tells me it will be
my joy.

It will be His gift to me,
and it will bubble over.
It will overflow.
It will be His love song
to the poor and broken hearted.

Carried along by the wind,
spreading seed
that will multiply,
a thousand times
what was sown.

The North

The Lord is near to all who call
on him... Psalms 145:18

I call on the Lord in my distress, and
he answers me. Psalms 120:1

Obstructed Labour

Power.
Passenger.
Passageway.
Psyche.

The four "P"s of obstructed labour.

Which has been the culprit here?
Who can I hold responsible for my frustrations?

Bitter

How can I tame this beast?
This dark thing,
this bitter thing,
this bile.
Its burn settles in my throat.
Its sting follows me.

How can I speak of beauty?
How can I dance?

My voice is hoarse;
my feet are bound.

I trip and stumble,
without grace.

12

It has been twelve years now,
and I remain—

a kinder lover,
a more gracious child,
a gentler mother.

I no longer scream at stone ceilings.

But my knuckles are bloodied
and raw
from flinging my hands
to heaven.

Even in my dreams
I have abandoned wildly.

Harden these bruised knees
harder still.

Let me speak with the
tongues of angels.

Heal the poor through my hands
and Your touch.

Bow me low to wash the feet
of Your children.

Make me hunger and thirst
for Your Word
and Your presence.

But sustain me with bread and wine,
for I am spent.

Done

Worn out
Weary
Drained
Exhausted
Tired
Fatigued
Spent
It seems I have so many terms
to describe this feeling,
yet so few
to describe its opposite—
or perhaps I am just too
Worn out
Weary
Drained
Exhausted
Tired
Fatigued
Spent
to think of them.

My Heart's Cry

Be with me here.
Closer.
Love me more,
in my distress,
in my wanting.

Understand me.
Rescue me.
Bind me to You.
Do not let me go.

Submission

Trying to make sense of this.
Learning to let it go.

To leave my palms open;
back bent or arched,
as the hour dictates.

I am the weeping willow;
I will flex to your need.

This is love—
without expectations.

In Pursuit of Purity

Restrain me.
Strip me of my rags.
Cleanse my wounds.
Touch the fiery coal
to my lips.

Let me hear the angels'
wings beating.
Fill my thoughts
with prophesy.

I will bind myself to You.
Dig my nails into the cross.
Hands blistered;
splinters deep.

But You have known
nails and thorns
much deeper still.

Take Me

Wanting home,
Father,
tonight.

To crawl out of this skin,
reach Your light
and rest.

Escape
the knowledge of pain,
my shortcomings;
resentment and bitterness.

These glimpses of you,
this longing,
pierces me through.

I am undone, Father.
Limp with exhaustion.
Shield me with your wings.

Heal me with oil and wine.
For I have been poured out;
surrendered.

Wanting your beauty,
like the brilliance of the sun.
Dare I ask?

O, to be pure of heart.

The Aching

This ache is big.
Stretched wide and tight;
like an animal hide to dry,
like the Alberta skies,
like the prairie fields,
like a drum-head.

It burns like the bright blistered skin of a scalded child.
It heaves with the apologetic retches of the wayward teen.
It gasps for the old man who struggles with each breath.

But You come to me
like a song.
Like a warm breeze.
Like the smell of spring.
Like chocolate.

And I am stilled.

The Cutting

They cut to feel something;
to numb the numbness.

Arms bloodied and raw,
staining paler lines.

Chalk marks on the prison wall.

I write to feel less.
This feeling is too much for me.
This ache threatens to split me in two.

The Withdrawal

The shakes are coming.
I can feel my cells starting to tremble.

My arteries pound out a song of distress.
My ligaments groan in their mourning.
My muscles echo,
and magnify the cry.
My skin crawls away.
My hair drowns in tears,
and sweat.

This is the withdrawal
that I have been dreading—
the separation of heart from soul,
the dissection of spirit from flesh.

My cadaver lies naked on display.
I am being dismembered.
My bones have been picked clean.

I lie on the altar of sacrifice.

Do not leave me.
Do not abandon your child.
Do not let this moment be denied,
unseen, unheard, unknown, unremembered.

Falling

I wish I could fly south
with the geese,
and these children
into the sun—
closer to You.

Brightened and beautiful;
purer than light.

But these roots are buried deep,
and with my efforts to withdraw,
only crack and break.

The birds are almost gone now,
chasing the sun.

So I try to encapsulate
and bury this ache.

Preparing for the silence;
the shortening of days.

I struggle to move, to dance,
but my motion is slowed
in this gelatinous air.

The tips of my fingers
yellow and fall—

Those who go out weeping,
carrying seeds to sow,

under this moon;
pregnant and pale.

will return with songs of joy,
carrying sheaves with them.

In the company of ravens,
I kneel prostrate
until my toes tingle.

I have lost the ability to circulate.

Send the rain to soften these lips—
dry from speaking in tongues.

Send the wind to tame me.

The phoenix
of my heart's fire
has taken flight.

And these ashes of my love
float suspended,
in the night sky,
ready to disperse.

Let the osmosis begin.

Psalms 126:6

The End of Autumn

Today the snow fell.

Large,
reluctant
flakes—
the first manifestation
of Fall's whispered threats.

Encouraging us to savour
these last days.

Denim skies—
a backdrop
to rust, gold, copper and wine.

And small boys insist
they are much too warm
for winter jackets.
There are stunts to perform
and battles to be won.

We race through long grass.
The wind burns my ears.

Stick swords are brandished
against unsuspecting mushrooms.
We've frightened the fungus
among us.

Forging ahead,
there is a silence,
a stillness.
Anticipation.
Nature is
waiting.

The birds have left already.
Perhaps the deer and moose are planning
some mysterious ritual
in preparation,
for this final celebration.

I both welcome
and dread
the graduation—
the inevitable changing of seasons.

But Nature shrugs
and settles.
Her work is done.
The farmers have harvested
their vast mazes of fallen grain.

And the fields lie patiently
like Aslan shorn;
awaiting the promise
of spring.

Forty Below

I'm becoming accustomed to
the snowness of things,
the bareness of here,
the bone coldness of this life.

Where the days
snap, crunch and dissolve
like icicles,
and white silhouettes white.

Where the air is dry and electric;
sounds muffled
by stillness.

The darkness illuminated only by stars
and these northern lights.

Come let us bury ourselves
under the quilt of winter.

It's time to hibernate.

We can spend our days in bed
and grow fat
on the spoils of our love.

Spring

The snow is starting to melt here.
The earth beginning its thaw,
and I am as muddied as the landscape.

Back arched,
arms stretched wide,
I close my eyes
and face the sun.
Searching for clarity.

No longer restrained by winter's frigid grip.
I long to sink my hands
deep into sun-warmed soil
and inhale.

Extracting vile fledgling weeds before their root systems establish.
I mourn as I clear the carcasses of Cold's casualties,
exclaim over stalwart survivors,
and indulge in Spring's catharsis.

Summer

Strawberry picking
today,
in the heat.

Picnic packed.
Hats, sunscreen, water, diapers.
Car seat straps adjusted,
A/C on,
and we're off.

Sandwiched between
fluorescent-yellow canola.
Romanced by the scent of wildflowers
and fresh tar.

We arrive—
amused by car doors left
open in the parking lot.
The risk of theft
deemed paltry;
weighed against returning
out of the frying pan,
into the fire.

Packed pails are picked up,
children are lifted up.
Thankful for a bit of a breeze,
bumping along on a dusty Gator back.

We return with fingertips and faces
sticky strawberry sweet,
cheeks bright from the heat,
hair wet with sweat.

Back in the car,
windows rolled down,
Dolly Parton competes
with the wind
for the serenade.

And perfectly packaged pods
are passed
to pacify
backseat pleas
for "peas please?"

Wish you were here.

Reflections

Canola fields inspire me.

Blatant brilliance;
unrestrained flattery
of the sun.

They radiate
their golden glory
recklessly.

And I am green with envy.
I wish I could love like that.

The South

He tends his flock like a shepherd: He gathers the lambs
in his arms and carries them close to his heart; he
gently leads those that have young. Isaiah 40:11

Then will the lame leap like a deer, and the mute
tongue shout for joy. Water will gush forth in the
wilderness and streams in the desert. Isaiah 35:6

Dreams in Green

Is this the place I've dreamed of?

Nights where the leaves shade leaves—
mingling, overlapping,
displaying the mystery of God's love
in variations of green.

The moss cushions me,
cradles these glass bones
as He whispers my name on the wind.

These days are just a shadow.
The first note in His love song.

I reach my arms to the sky
and wait for the dance to begin.

How do I love?

The sun
the rain
the cold
the heat
this pen
this paper
these hands
these feet
the word
the wine
the work
the rest
and you.

On Growing of Moss

He is teaching me,
how the earth moves,
how the bud blooms,
how the seasons change,
how the sun sets,
how the fog shifts,
how the dog howls,
how the leaves fall,
how the moss grows.

One

I have become one.
The embodiment of His love.

I am being transformed.

My limbs are beginning to bud.
My hair twists into vines.
The graft of this branch has taken hold.

My lips drip with honey.
Dates and figs fall from my fingers.
I breathe apples into existence.
My hands cup the dew.

Listen to His song.
It is sweetness itself.
Rest in His shade,
as the noon sun beats down.

His abundance is enough.
It is all that will satisfy.

Eve's Child

Eve's youngest daughter,
I have not yet learned,
the secret
of satisfaction.

I have lent my ear
to the serpent's tongue.

Teach me to see Eden,
in this desert.
Lead me through
this valley.

Heal these broken legs,
not just to walk but
to dance.

Burn the scales off my eyes
with Your pillar of fire.
I want to see Your holiness.

Sing to me again
the song of Your love.

For I have tasted
the fruit of Your vineyard
and it is good.

Break Through

Choose life
tight ball
of vulnerability.
Let your tender petals unfurl.
Let your bruised lips open.
Let your raw heart pulse
with hope.

Reach up,
through
cracked ground.
Push your limbs
through the dust.
Stretch
into
your
fullness
of being.

Let the Creator
breathe new life
into your lungs—
and inhale.
Let his Spirit
fill you
and overflow.

Send shoots.
Release vines.
Lavish love.
Burst into abundance.

Wrench weights of worry.
Shed shackles of shame.
Cut chains of condemnation.
Be imprisoned
and imprison
no more.

Break through
the rubble.
Turn your face
to the sun.
Grow beyond the
rocks, weeds, worms, decay.

Step into the miracle
of transformation.

When you choose to bury the
choking, crushing, shading, stunting
words of the wounded,
in the Creator's hand
and wait—
He will redeem.

And you will thrive.

Kneeling

We are led to this.
Drawn to the edge.
Frayed and raw.

Bound too tight
by expectations and frustrations,
burdens and grief.

We are weary,
and long for relief, release.
Hear us,
and send the Comforter.

Let us know the presence
of Your Spirit.
Heal us—
that we may continue to heal.

We are overwhelmed
by sorrow.
Daily we are exposed.

Guide our thoughts,
our lips,
our hands.

Shine Your light,
that we may see
Your path
laid bare.

Pilgrims

We walk—
bleary eyed,
foggy headed,
stumbling under the sun.

Feet calloused,
blisters tender,
we drag our burdens behind us
and clutch tight
our worries and woes.

Holding them close to our chest.
We treasure them.
Deceived by the illusion
that this poison
is precious.

But He calls us tenderly
to release our white knuckle grasp;
to let Him cleanse our wounds,
with His tears.

He invites us
to let Him
untie our burdens
and wash our feet.

Free.
Scrubbed clean
of grit and grime.

We will run with arms spread wide
and our faces will shine
with His glory!

Common

This common condition
finds us
off centre—
imbalanced.

Unaware that our focus is blurred.
So accustomed to this lotus land.

Befuddled, spun 'round, mesmerized.
We walk drunkenly.
Not seeing how we stagger.
Not realizing how lines have blurred.

How taking the lion's share,
is wounding the lambs.

Lord, make our hearts tender.
Soften us.
Bring the tears,
that will wash away mountains.

Make our bodies shake,
with sobs that will shatter
this prison of greed.

Rescue us from mediocrity.
We have been lulled
into complacency.

Make us examples
of humility
and selflessness,
carrying torches of hope.
Teach us Your ways.

Children of the King

Help us to see ourselves
for what we are—

greedy,
selfish,
insecure,
arrogant,
and children of the King.

We compete for crumbs;
while your banquet awaits.
Enamoured by evil;
while Your glory shines.

Release our grasp on our
chains of wealth—
that we may hold Your hand.

Open our eyes to
see Your gifts.
Open our minds to
understand Your word.
Open our hearts to
receive Your love.

Let us long to hear
Your voice,
more than our own.

*"Let the one who boasts
boast in the Lord"*

2 Corinthians 10:17

Created

Each cell of your body
has been created
with a purpose.
Imagined and formed by the Creator of the universe.
Loved in every detail of their complexity;
the microscopic parts of you hold hands
and join to form something worthy of amazement.
Functional and beautiful—
you are an example of His glory.
Unfathomably intricate,
fascinating,
miraculous;
full of potential for good.
This is who you were made to be.

Relax.

You are wonderful already.

You are already blessed—
because He loves you.
You don't need to fight for it.
You don't need to earn it.

Look at Him.
He wants to show you Himself.
He is the answer to all of your questions.
He is the solution to all of your problems.

Give it up.

Release it—
bitterness,
fear,
anger,
pride,
jealousy.

Make room in your heart.
He will set you free.

Hope

These fingerprints are unique.
Specifically designed
to leave their imprint
on this sphere.

These hands hold
no exceptional strength
or dexterity,
yet have been moulded
to heal hearts.

The hearts of ordinary people;
that live ordinary lives.
Carrying around in them
so much secret hurt
and private shame.

Pretending they are strong;
the show must go on.

And they plod through their days
with concrete feet.
Not realizing that this bravado
is a barrier to health.
This wall of protection
makes them blind.

Open their eyes Lord.
Open their hearts,
to receive healing.
They need You so desperately,
but are afraid to ask;

afraid of more rejection,
more criticism,
more abuse.

Make me a conduit
of comfort.
Let them see,
You are safe.
You long to heal.

None of these secrets
are secret from You.

We place our hope in You.

Searching for

the beauty in the ashes;
the sweetness in the bitter;
the triumph in the tragedy;
the victory in the war.

Through
the denial
the withholding
the storing in
the pouring out
the nailing down
the tearing up.

With my eyes shut tight-wide open;
with my fists clenched-fingers spread;
with my face to the heavens;
with my knees on the ground.

On Edge

I see you beautiful boy-man,
walking the edge of the wave.

Like Peter on the way
to his Savior—
half soaring/half sinking.

Like a finger along
the blade of a knife.
Holding your breath—
to see if you bleed.

Know this beautiful boy-man,
you are seen,
you are known,
you are fully understood,
by the One who calms the waves
and heals the wound of the knife.

Even When, Even While.

Even when the rooster
crows thrice,
with a wink of the eye
and the scuff of a claw,
to seal our fate—
Jesus has chosen to forgive.

Even while
we deny
we know Him,
He reaches down;
to pull us from the pit.

He lays His body down,
as the bridge to our salvation.

Wide eyed

Peace

He that is in you,
is greater than he that is in the world.

Joy

I have overcome.
I am the answer.
I am the source of all healing,
and I do not want to withhold it.

Reach out.
Don't deny Me
with your competence.
I use the incompetent.
I use the willing.
I use the humble.

Be present.
Listen.
Be aware.
Speak the words I give you.
Place your hands as I instruct you.

Watch and be amazed!

There is

There is One
who can go with you
down to the depths.

One who the gates of hell
cannot prevail against.

He can rescue you
and bring you home.

Take His hand;
He can be trusted.

He can handle your pain;
it won't overwhelm Him.

He is the perfect manifestation
of strength
and gentleness.

His power
brings mountains to their knees
and makes the clouds weep.

His caress
created the wing of the butterfly
and the petal of the crocus.

Our Shelter in Suffering

How can we breathe?
How can our hearts keep beating?
How can we put one foot in front of the other?

And yet the sun rises
and yet the birds sing
and yet the flowers bloom.

Lord we reach for Your promises,
"Blessed are those who mourn
for they will be comforted."

Come to us in our grief.
We need You near.
Wrap us tightly in Your arms.
Hold us close in our distress.
Hear our groaning.

We need reassurance of Your unfailing love.
We need to see Your beauty in this pain.

Daddy!
This hurts!
We ache!
Our hearts are broken.

We can't do this without you.
Come to our rescue.
Be our help.

Matthew 5:4

See our tears!
Hear our cries!

We need You to be our Shepherd.
We wander aimlessly without You.

Guide us.
Be our comfort.
Shelter us in Your wings.

Blessed be the name of the Lord.

Joy

God invites us,
in our brokenness, weakness and pain
to draw close to Him;
to take comfort and rest in the shelter of His wings.
Yet the greatest blessing,
is that it is in this place, that we are close enough to hear His heartbeat.
And the song that it sings is love;
love for you but also love for those around you;
those that you bump up against every day.
He wants you to be able to hear this, because this is what will bring healing.
This is what will bring reconciliation.
Your goal doesn't need to be to do anything,
except be willing to humble yourself to come to Him.
When your heart lives so close to his
then it supernaturally becomes stronger and healthier
and its rhythm starts to beat with His.
This is what will bring you true joy;
joy that is irrespective of circumstances;
joy that is contagious.

Warrior Monk

There are times when I wish
I could become a monk;
spend my days
on my knees
in prayer.

Plant some seeds.
Pull some weeds.
Bake some bread.
Sing
and pray.

What intimacy with the Father!
Heaven on earth
and yet;

I am surrounded by agony.
I can hear it.
I can feel their ache.

Deep groanings to the Father—
Rescue us!
Save us!
Send someone to bind up our wounds!
Hear our cries!

What choice do I have but to go?

Of the Moon and of Mourning

Numberless nights
three quarters awake—
walking and wailing,
eclipsed,
by kneeling and weeping,
for one less restless
in the nest.

Grief a half circle,
half mirrored/half hidden,
in the black hole of night.

Now waxing,
Now waning,
Now streaming,
Now shaking.

Fists at the moon,
elbows sanding the floor.

The new is not full.
The full is now empty.
Now empty is new.
Is the new empty?
The new empty is now.

Fall's Shadow

I have seen Fall's shadow.

It sneaks its way in
on
tip
toe.

When my back is turned
I notice the angle of the sun
has shifted
just so
the light shines
thin
and blue.

With my anxieties on its heels;
it creeps
silently at first.

And then the whispers grow;
with the chilling of toes;
with the blowing of winds;
with the darkening of days;
with the lengthening of nights.

You Are
Not
Enough.

Earth Weds Spring

A dense emerald carpet glistens and waves;
punctuated by bleating puffs of black and grey.

Families of pale yellow trumpets sway on slim stalks,
while cedars present offerings of
fragrant olive lace.

Blushing pink pom poms drop petals of confetti
and tiny transparent spades shine green—
like heaven's stained glass.

"Alone" in the Forest

Aspens with moss stockings
lean on tiptoes to kiss
across the path.

Young ferns curl shyly
like dainty violin scrolls;
like can-can dancers preparing to kick.

Horse hoofprints
make shallow pools to reflect the sun.

Velvet bunnies
bounce
spring
hop!

Tiny pinecones twirl in the breeze
and bees hum a melody,

while solemn brown owls
conduct the jubilee.

I am a witness to nature's ballet!

Soccer

We watch
blotchy faced teens
rush,
flushed,
fresh sweat flies.

Dogs lie
warm
in the sun—

ignorant of the week's
accumulated hormones
expelled
in the running
back
and forth
steaming out

on this Saturday
afternoon stress test.

Parents savour sitting,
hoping mouths and minds
leave purified.

At the Sea

Seagulls soar,
weaving back and forth;
like cars in traffic;
like yarn in a loom.

They eye the ocean's offerings—
flame hued exoskeletons
lying half shattered in the sand;
already picked clean of their treasures.

Young boys scramble up sand bluffs
scattered with poppies,
like drops of blood.

The dog leads and follows,
trying to anticipate
where excitement will strike next.

The wind whips waves;
salting the air;
preserving memories.

The In-Between Spaces

*Take my yoke upon you and learn from me,
for I am gentle and humble in heart, and you
will find rest for your souls. Matthew 11:29*

*But the wisdom that comes from heaven is
first of all pure; then peace-loving, considerate,
submissive, full of mercy and good fruit,
impartial and sincere. James 3:17*

Mexico

This is the start, mi amiga!

We have laid arms, legs, torsos bare.
The sea and sun will not disappoint.

Our systematic sunscreen application
will not hinder
their mission to purify;
to disinfect this past year.

Black birds beckon,
like glistening obsidian;
omnipresent oracles
of optimism.

Blossoming buds burst
into brightest blooms—
hues of hurray!

Geckos galavant gleefully;
inviting intoxicated iguana
basking blissfully
on vibrant walls.

Even the fruits and fishes
conscript and conspire
to satisfy
both hunger and thirst;

to replace
the memory of fasts
with feasts.

This is the season of healing;
of somersaults in salt water.

Italy

Lessons we learned
as we laboured
in the land of love—

the love of work
and the work of love.

Olives
on ancient
trees
grey green,
whisper wisdom
to the grass.

The birds listen for echoes
from
brick to stone
and join the chant.

The chorus intensifies—

Delight in the wine!
Savour rich cheeses, sweet tomatoes and oil!
Inhale the scent of espresso!

Harken to the honey of history,
this is no time for smallness.

We are surrounded by the grandeur
of cathedrals
with windows of stained glass.

Can we learn to live
as warriors of love?

Will these monasteries protect us?

We look instead to the sky.

The Wooing

Bring the sound of My heart
to these people.
Let them hear its rhythm.
Let them dance to its beat.

It is the sound of joy.
It is the voice of My love.
Each note is meant to woo them.
Each chord was designed to
draw them near.

Let My music surround them.
Let it comfort them in their distress.
Let it invite them to worship.
Let it inspire them to shine.

My love for them is so big!
I will go to any length to reach them.
I will tear down mountains.
I will break through walls.

My children will know that
their Father has not forsaken them;
My hand is still strong to save them.

St. Paul's Orphans

Orientation to a rotation
in sorrow.

Our Father's children
have been abused
and abandoned.

Deceived by the liar
and thief of this world;
souls sold
for fool's gold.

Bodies tattooed by trauma;
bruised and battered;
beauty stolen by a lie.

Wasted limbs lie
weakened;
strength spent
fighting demons
in angels' clothing.

Reflections on Bacteremia

Yellow gowned and gloved
we float
from room
to room—

a gaggle of ghosts
purposed to purge plasma
of its pathogens.

The glorious Staph aureus
has struck—
again.

Were it not so sinister
we would praise
its persistence.

Penetrating bone to marrow;
passages forged through blood;
it targets the heart.

How can we win?
Combat the villain
with Cloxacillin!

What?
It's MRSA they say—
Vancomycin
will save the day!

We sway;
composing hymns
of acronyms.

For the Seekers of Refuge

Welcome!
Bienvenue!

to this land
of heart healing
beauty.

Watch
the ocean
wash away
your tears.

Let
the wind
woo
your weary mind.

Climb
the hills
to the forests
of forgiveness.

Tell
your secrets
to the trees.

Breathe
the fragrance of
freedom.

Walk
into the promise

of a new life.

Now is your time to lean. To wrap your arms around the necks of your foreign brothers and sisters. Let us lend you our shoulders for a time. Let us carry you off the battle field. We are so sorry to hear of your grief. Our hearts are here and open. We want to help cushion your landing. How long your journey has been to get here! How unfamiliar and overwhelming these surroundings must be! Let us speak the common language of compassion. Let us share with you from our excess. We have more than enough. Welcome to our family.

The foreigner residing among you must be treated as your native-born. Love them as yourself, for you were foreigners in Egypt. I am the Lord your God. Leviticus 19:34

Kenya

What makes this earth
brown red and
red brown
crumple up
tumble down?

Big heart throbbing.
Pulsing.
Heaving.
Bursting.

So alive.
So rich.
But full of grief.

Overwhelming.
Passionate.
Sadness.

It is the laugh
that lasts so long,
it turns to a cry.

It is that deep place,
where the soul
hits the ground.

It is the place
of mourning
for shattered dreams
and lost children.

Can I walk with you there?
Will you put your hand in mine?

As we with hands held
look to the Creator;
with prayers that
His spirit
will meet us here,
with a song of
redemption.

That the planting of
this deep sorrow
in this place that is
crumpled up
and tumbled down;
will bring the most beautiful
new fruit to life.

In this earth that is
brown red and
red brown.

Soul Salve

Into the heart
of the pearl
of Africa, we go.

Distanced briefly
from the thin arms
and fevered flesh
of our black-skinned
brothers and sisters.

We embark on a journey
into the lush abundance
of tropical
fields and forests.

Seeking answers
among tall grass
and trees
with twisted
trunks.

Heeding hefty hippos
snoozing submerged
beneath ancient papyrus.

We search the savannah
for salvation.

What truths have
elated elephants entombed?
Buried.

Fermenting.
Awaiting the perfection of time.

Learning lessons from lounging lions.
Scorning the bloated body
of prey offered,
without a hunt.

We survey a stretched swollen snake lying roadside.
Overfull.
Inert and immobilized
by gluttony.

Glimpse
gangly
giraffes.
Long
necked
lovers.
Reaching
above
the
common
satisfaction.

And watch wallowing warthogs.
Cooling hides
in shallow mud,
gorgeously ugly.

What a wonder—
the privilege we have
in this wounded nation.
And a calling—

to bend forward
toward healing.

Sharing in Nature's balm
to salve souls.

The Returning

For the revelation awaits an appointed time; it speaks to the end and will not prove false. Though it linger, wait for it; it will certainly come and will not delay. Habbakkuk 2:3

I have loved you with an everlasting love; I have drawn you with loving-kindness. Jeremiah 31:3

Salinity

Take me.
Plunge me down
beneath the waters
of Your sea.

Submerge me deep
into the blue.
Pull me near—
closer
to You.

I want to hear the silence.
I long to feel the cool.
I need to know the dark.

I ache
to be alone
with You.

Rocked beneath the waves—
anchored to your heart.
Satiate my soul
with the salt
of You.

Fill me.
Surround me.
Wash me away.
Dissolve this fear
of drowning.

Baptize me
with Your promise
of rebirth.

Good Shepherd

Legs crumpled
under,
wool matted and mud stained.
These weakened limbs lie still,
resigned.
There is no fight left.
Resisting the elements
has left me humbled.

Hungry and hurting.
Bruised and bedraggled.
Wounded and wolf weary.

And then I hear the Shepherd's voice
"Lie still, my child.
You don't need to thrash
like a wild animal.
You can trust me;
I will gather you up."

And as he lifts me,
I can feel His breath
on my face.
And I can hear
His heart throbbing.
And I can hear His Spirit
and He's singing;
and the song is freedom
and beauty and joy.

He is my healing.
He is my promise.

My green pastures.
My quiet waters.
He will anoint my head with oil.
He will restore my soul.

God's Response
to my Misplaced Affection

Oh my child,
don't you see?
I love you more
always so much more
than the world does.

I am enraptured by your beauty.
I am thrilled by your wonderful uniqueness.
I esteem the true value of your worth.
I treasure you because I made you.
You are so precious to me.

Nothing that you do,
or don't do,
will ever change that.

I am the author of the story of love.

I am the
most beautiful,
most wealthy,
most powerful,
most wise,
most kind,
and I love you the most.

I created and I own the entire earth.
Everything that I do is with you in mind.

I want to bring you close to me.
I want to hold you in my arms.

I want to whisper in your ear.
I want to walk with you in the garden.

Don't believe the snake.
He is full of jealousy and hate.
He is the author of lies.

He wants you to believe that I don't love you and that I am not
beautiful or wealthy or powerful or wise or kind— but it is a lie.

He wants to entice you
away from me,
because he is evil,
but don't be fooled!

He comes only
to steal
and to kill
and to destroy.

Keep your eyes
looking directly
into my eyes.
You will see
that they are full
of love and compassion.

I adore you.

Don't look to things to bring you joy.
Moths and rust will destroy them.
This world will soon pass away.
A new world is coming.

Love your brothers and sisters;
but don't expect them to complete you.
Only I can do that;
they stumble just like you.

Hold my hand.
I am strong.
I love you
and I know the way.

Branded

I have been branded.
His name pressed into my flesh.
His signature tattooed on the palms of my hands.
I have been marked by the Maker.
A child of God.

Sealed with His stamp.
Monogramed by Mystery.

Face radiant—
though veiled.
I cannot deny
my encounter
with the Holy One.
I cannot reject
my right hand.

He has formed me from dust.
He has moulded me from clay.
He has wrought me from iron.

In the dark spaces.
In the blinding light.
In the holding up.
In the pounding down.
In the melting.
In the making.
Allowing Him to glow.

In the Refiner's fire,
sparks fly—
the sword is reborn as a spade;
the spear reformed as shears.

A weapon of war
now a tool of restoration.
Planting hope where there was none.
Pruning patiently in preparation.
In expectation—
of *love, joy, peace, patience, kindness, goodness, faithfulness, gentleness
and self-control.*

Galatians 5:22

Beloved

Beloved
He calls me.
He tells me I am His,
and it is the very best way of belonging.

He tells me
He wants all of me,
even the parts
that I don't want to share—
the giving that is heart breaking.

My Savior is craving
my heart and my soul
and my mind and my strength—
little though it be.

He says I am never hidden.
He will always pursue me
with passion,
jealous and fierce,
bold and relentless
in the hunt
for my heart.

He wants me to come to Him
in my distress,
in my longing,
in my waiting,
in my wanting,
in my singing,
in my celebrating.

My loyal guardian,
He will never abandon me—
for I am His.

Though I may be
rejected,
shamed,
scorned,
neglected.

He always protects,
always trusts,
always hopes,
always perseveres—
His love never fails.

He is trying to woo me,
to draw me to Him,
with leaves that glow like flames;
with the touch of His breath on my skin;
with the sound of thunder;
with the sweetness of sugar;
with the smell of the sea.

How can I resist?
What can compete with communion
with the King?

Acknowledgements

It is no small task to express gratitude to the individuals who have helped to shape a collection of poems written over so many years. I have been taught, supported and inspired in immeasurable ways, by so many.

I pray that these poems point the way to a Saviour who sees you, knows you and longs to have a relationship with you.

I am thrilled to be able to include the beautiful illustrations by the talented Talia Ball. It has been a privilege to work with you. And to all the staff at WestBow publishing, thank you for your forbearance with a self publishing newbie.

Beginning from the start of this journey, I would like to thank the staff and my fellow physicians at the former Associate Medical Clinic of Peace River and the Peace River Community Health Centre. What a wonderful welcome our family had to this beautiful community. I am so grateful for the understanding and patient encouragement that was provided to me as a freshly graduated resident. I had so much to learn and I will never forget the grace that was shown, as I took my first wobbly steps into a new life.

To the staff and my fellow physicians at the Town Circle Medical Clinic, I would like to express my sincere gratitude for the inspiration that you each were to me. Your compassion, wisdom and diligent dedication to our patients, were a consistent example of what excellent medical care looks like.

To the staff and my fellow physicians at St Joseph's Hospital and the North Island Hospital Comox Valley, I am so appreciative of the ways that you have come alongside me over the years. Through, at times, bafflingly complex patient presentations; frustrating barriers to care; mind numbing work hours and heart wrenching experiences, I have known that I was not alone. That there was a team working with me, each individual contributing their precious talents, skills and training to provide healing and comfort to patients, was such an encouragement to me.

To the people I have met and worked with in far off places: Pamoja, Tanzania; Kijabe Hospital, Kenya; Gulu Regional Referral Hospital, Uganda; Watoto Suubi, Uganda— you have left an indelible imprint on me. The passion for the poor and the persistence in doing good; despite limited resources and huge challenges; that I have seen demonstrated in these places, is a model of Christ's love.

To my patients, I am in awe of your openness, honesty and resilience. I have learned so much from you, thank you.

To my life long friends and travelling companions—Dawn Petten and Martina Scholtens, thank you for all of the adventures. Your friendship is one of my most precious gifts.

To Jenny Rohne, who has graciously adopted us into her ever growing family, thank you for all the wonderful introductions, including my amazing women's bible study group. Having a group of women to teach me, listen to me, pray with me and cheer me on, has been such an incredible blessing. It has been an example of the love and power of "*him who is able to do immeasurably more than we ask or imagine.*" Ephesians 3:10

To my friends faraway, Stephanie Forder and Becky Joe, what a treat it has been to be able to keep in touch, despite our distances and differences. I love the perspectives you share and your incredible love for your families. I strive to love better because of you.

To my confidant and counsellor, Jean Boylan, your insight and words of wisdom, have been invaluable. Thank you for your prayers and for speaking truth with gentleness.

To my church family at Comox Pentecostal Church, your faithful service to the family of God and our community is a practical demonstration of our calling to be ministers of reconciliation. Thank you for your grace and ongoing support.

To my mom, Fran Mosey, the one who first introduced me to Jesus, lover of my soul, thank you. There has been no greater gift given.

To the Gregory family, thank you for your love, forgiveness and acceptance. We are so grateful for your abundant generosity and selfless hospitality.

To my husband Jacob and sons—Elijah, Jonah and Zeke, thank you for holding my hands and walking this road with me. Your unique personalities, interests, and gifts are such a treasure. What an honor to be able to learn to love with you.

And to the Alpha and Omega, I am so thankful that You have been and always will be with me on the journey. Communion with You is nothing less than life sustaining, bread and wine.

Printed in the United States
By Bookmasters